W9-BQY-050

ELON MUSK

ELON MUSK

Tesla Founder and Titan of Tech

MARGARET J. GOLDSTEIN

Lerner Publications ◆ Minneapolis

Lerner Publications Company
An imprint of Lerner Publishing Group, Inc.
241 First Avenue North
Minneapolis, MN 55401 USA

For reading levels and more information, look up this title at www.lernerbooks.com.

Image credits: dpa picture alliance/Alamy Stock Photo, p. 2; Xinhua/Alamy Stock Photo, p. 6; AP Photo/John Raoux, p. 8; Finn stock/Shutterstock.com, p. 10; Tinxi/Shutterstock.com, p. 11; JHVEPhoto/Shutterstock.com, p. 13; Uladzik Kryhin/Shutterstock.com, p. 15; REUTERS/ Jonathan Ernst/Alamy Stock Photo, p. 16; AP Photo/Paul Sakuma, p. 17; AP Photo/Jae C. Hong, p. 18; AP Photo/The Santa Maria Times, Leah Thompson, p. 19; AP Photo/Remy de la Mauviniere, p. 21; AP Photo/Mark Von Holden, p. 22; NASA, pp. 24, 31; AP Photo/Reed Saxon, p. 27; AP Photo/Dave Bedrosian/Geisler-Fotopress/picture-alliance/dpa, p. 28; AP Photo/Evan Agostini/Invision, p. 29; NASA/Bill Ingalls, p. 32; AP Photo/Robyn Beck/Pool Photo, p. 34; AP Photo/Refugio Ruiz, p. 36; NASA/CASE FOR MARS, p. 38; NASA/JSC/SpaceX, p. 39; NASA/ KSC/SpaceX, p. 40. Cover image: AP Photo/Jae C. Hong.

Main body text set in Rotis Serif Std 55 Regular. Typeface provided by Adobe Systems.

Editor: Brianna Kaiser

Library of Congress Cataloging-in-Publication Data

Names: Goldstein, Margaret J., author.
Title: Elon Musk : Tesla founder and titan of tech / Margaret J. Goldstein.
Description: Minneapolis : Lerner Publications , 2022. | Series: Gateway biographies | Includes bibliographical references and index. | Audience: Ages 9–14 | Audience: Grades 4–6 | Summary: "Born in South Africa in 1971, young Elon Musk loved inventions. He later founded Tesla, SpaceX, and the company that would become PayPal. Read about how Musk became one of the world's most famous entrepreneurs"– Provided by publisher.
Identifiers: LCCN 2020028313 (print) | LCCN 2020028314 (ebook) | ISBN 9781728404462 (library binding) | ISBN 9781728418179 (ebook)
Subjects: LCSH: Musk, Elon–Juvenile literature. | SpaceX (Firm)–Juvenile literature. | Tesla Motors–Juvenile literature. | Businesspeople–United States–Biography–Juvenile literature.
Classification: LCC HC102.5.M88 G65 2022 (print) | LCC HC102.5.M88 (ebook) | DDC 338.092 [B]–dc23

LC record available at https://lccn.loc.gov/2020028313
LC ebook record available at https://lccn.loc.gov/2020028314

Manufactured in the United States of America
1-48504-49018-4/19/2021

TABLE OF CONTENTS

Boy Wonder   9

Fast Company   14

Electric Storm   19

Blast Off!   23

Reaching for the Stars   31

Idea Man   33

Rule Breaker   38

Important Dates   42
Source Notes   44
Selected Bibliography   46
Learn More   47
Index   48

Musk gives a presentation at Tesla Design Studio in 2015.

On February 6, 2018, thousands of spectators crowded the roads and beaches near Kennedy Space Center in Merritt Island, Florida. They had come to watch a rocket blast into space. The giant vehicle, which was taller than a twenty-story building, towered above the launchpad. During liftoff, the rocket's engines roared, and vast clouds of dark smoke billowed into the air. The rocket lifted into the clear daytime sky, a giant tail of flames following behind.

As the rocket climbed steadily upward, the crowd pointed and cheered. Inside the Kennedy Space Center control room, dozens of aerospace engineers, rocket technicians, and mission controllers clapped and celebrated. The team worked for the aerospace company SpaceX. The rocket they had successfully launched that day, the Falcon Heavy, was one of the most powerful rockets of all time.

Most rockets that blast off from Earth carry satellites, supplies for the International Space Station (ISS), space probes, space telescopes, or other scientific equipment. But the Falcon Heavy rocket carried an unusual payload, or cargo: a shiny, cherry-red Roadster, a sports car made by Tesla. Playing on the Roadster's sound system as it shot into space was the song "Space Oddity" by David Bowie. And sitting in the car's driver's seat was a dummy wearing a white space suit and a space helmet. The team at SpaceX gave another nod to David Bowie by naming the dummy after his song "Starman."

Smoke billows into the sky as the Falcon Heavy launches into space on February 6, 2018.

Shooting a sports car into space might sound like a crazy idea, but not to anyone familiar with SpaceX and Tesla. The two companies had something in common: Elon Musk was the chief executive officer (CEO). Since the first decade of the 2000s, Musk had been breaking barriers in both the aerospace and the automobile industries. He was also at the forefront of other world-changing technology, such as solar power and artificial intelligence (AI). The launch of a Tesla sports car on a SpaceX rocket was not just a publicity stunt. It was also a celebration of Musk's achievements.

Boy Wonder

Errol Musk, a mechanical and electrical engineer, and Maye Haldeman Musk, a fashion model and dietician, had three children. Their oldest child, Elon Reeve Musk, was born on June 28, 1971. Elon's brother, Kimbal, was born in 1972, and his sister, Tosca, was born in 1974. The Musk family lived in Pretoria in South Africa, a nation at the southern tip of the African continent.

Elon was a quiet and brainy boy. He loved reading, especially science fiction, fantasy, and stories about space travel. After school, he hung out at the local bookstore. On the weekends, he sometimes read two books in a day. His mom even called him "the encyclopedia" because he was always reading and absorbing information.

When Elon was eight years old, his parents separated. At first, he and his siblings lived with their mom in Durban, South Africa. But about two years later, Elon and Kimbal went to live with their dad in Johannesburg. Their dad taught them many engineering basics, such as how to run electrical wires into a house and how to install plumbing. "I'm naturally good at engineering . . . because I inherited it from my father," Musk said many years later. "What's very difficult for others is easy for me. For a while, I thought [mechanical and electrical] things were so obvious that everyone must know this." Elon's dad also taught him how to mix together chemicals to make explosives. Elon and Kimbal used that knowledge to build their own toy rockets, made of canisters filled with gunpowder.

Musk lived with his dad in Johannesburg, South Africa. South Africa is Africa's southernmost country.

At the age of ten, Elon saw a personal computer (PC) for the first time in an electronics store. With his saved allowance, and with the help of his dad, he bought his first PC, a Commodore VIC-20. The machine came with instructions for programming in the BASIC computer language. Elon studied the book and mastered the instructions in three days. In 1984 twelve-year-old Elon used the PC to create code for a sci-fi computer game, which he called *Blastar*. A South African computer magazine paid him $500 for the code and published it for readers. The introduction in the magazine explained, "In this game you have to destroy an alien space freighter, which is carrying deadly Hydrogen Bombs and Status Beam Machines."

Musk's first computer was a Commodore VIC-20.

Elon's middle school years were hard for him. He was small, the youngest kid in his grade, and was bullied. He got through those tough years by putting his attention into learning more about computers. In high school, he continued to learn coding, mastering not only BASIC but also the COBOL and Pascal computer languages.

After graduating from high school, Musk enrolled at the University of Pretoria, where he studied engineering and physics. But by then he was hoping to leave South Africa. Silicon Valley, an area south of San Francisco, California, was the heart of the emerging personal computer industry. Musk hoped to work there someday, and he made a plan. His mother had grown up in Canada and was a Canadian citizen. That connection meant that Musk could become a Canadian citizen too. He decided to move to Canada as a first step and then move to its southern neighbor, the United States.

He moved to Canada in 1989 and lived with some cousins for a time. After working at a few odd jobs, he enrolled at Queen's University in Kingston, Ontario. His brother later followed in his footsteps by leaving South Africa and enrolling at the same university. In his spare time, Musk built computers from scratch and sold them to other students for less than they'd have to pay for store-bought machines. He earned additional money by fixing computers. During his two years at Queen's University, Musk met fellow student Justine Wilson, who wanted to become a writer. The two began dating.

After leaving South Africa for Canada, Musk studied at Queen's University in Kingston, Ontario.

In 1992 Musk transferred to the University of Pennsylvania in Philadelphia. He chose the school for its top-notch reputation. Finally, he was able to move to the United States. Wilson remained in Canada, and the two had a long-distance relationship. At Penn, Musk continued to work hard and learn more about business and science. He impressed one professor with a paper on solar energy and solar power plants. He described a way to capture the sun's energy using solar collectors in space. He envisioned enormous devices, 2.5 miles (4 km) wide, sending solar energy to Earth via microwaves. In another paper, Elon wrote about ultracapacitors, devices that could store power for cars, airplanes, and rockets. He graduated from Penn with two bachelor's degrees, in physics and economics.

Fast Company

During the summer of 1994, Musk finally got to Silicon Valley. He interned with Pinnacle Research Institute in Los Gatos, California. The company was working on a project that Musk already knew something about: using ultracapacitors in electric vehicles. He also interned at Rocket Science Games, which made video games with dazzling special effects. Musk's job there was to write computer code, but he often tackled extra work beyond his assigned tasks.

After graduating from Penn, Musk enrolled in a PhD program in engineering at Stanford University. This Silicon Valley–area school was a hub for the computer revolution in the 1990s, including brand-new internet communications. But after only a few days as a Stanford student, he realized that he didn't want to be in school studying technology. He wanted to be out in the business world, running his own technology company. He quit the PhD program.

Many technology companies have their headquarters in Silicon Valley. Musk moved there in 1994.

His brother joined him in California, and in 1995 the two launched Global Link Information Network, later renamed Zip2. Funded by investors, the company produced online city directories with business listings and maps to help consumers find stores and services. The business prospered. When the computer company Compaq offered to buy Zip2 in 1999, the brothers sold it. Musk used part of his $22 million payout to start another business, X.com, an online banking company. He enjoyed his newfound wealth, buying a $1 million

Musk (*left*) and Kimbal Musk (*right*) started Global Link Information Network in 1995. Here, the brothers attend an event in 2020.

McLaren sports car and his own small airplane, which he learned to fly. In 2000 X.com merged with the online payment company Confinity, and the business was renamed PayPal. When eBay bought PayPal for $1.5 billion in 2002, once again Musk profited handsomely. This time, his payout was more than $150 million.

By then Wilson had joined Musk in California. The two married in 2000. After the sale of PayPal, they left Silicon Valley for Los Angeles. Musk had been interested in rockets and space travel since childhood. He hoped to work in the aerospace industry, which had a strong base in LA.

In Los Angeles, Musk learned about an organization that wanted to build a human colony on Mars. He loved the idea and ran with it. He devised a project, dubbed Mars Oasis, to send a private spacecraft to Mars. The spaceship would carry robotic greenhouses for growing plants on the Martian surface. As they grew, the plants would release oxygen, which would make the air on Mars breathable

Musk (*right*) and PayPal cofounder Peter Thiel (*left*) pose with the PayPal logo in 2000.

for future human colonists. Determined to carry out this plan, Musk and two colleagues traveled to Russia three times between 2001 and 2002 to try to buy the rocket they needed to launch a spacecraft. They met with Russian aerospace executives but came home each time without a deal. But Musk wasn't about to give up. He told his colleagues, "Hey, guys. I think we can build this rocket ourselves."

Musk teamed up with aerospace engineer Tom Mueller, who shared his interest in rocketry. At that time, only enormous companies built rockets. The biggest aerospace firms were Lockheed Martin and Boeing. They did business with the US National Aeronautics and Space Administration (NASA) and other government agencies. These wealthy firms employed tens of thousands of workers and secured multibillion-dollar government contracts. Their big, powerful rockets launched large satellites as well as space probes. Musk and Mueller saw a way to compete with these big firms. They envisioned a company that would build smaller, more efficient, and more affordable rockets to launch smaller payloads into space. In June 2002 they founded Space Exploration Technologies, or SpaceX, in El Segundo, California.

SpaceX, originally located in El Segundo, has its headquarters in Hawthorne, California.

Since starting SpaceX, Musk (*left*) keeps coming up with new ideas. Here, he talks to California governor Gavin Newsom about plans for the Falcon Heavy.

Along with a new company, Musk had a new family member. His son, Nevada Alexander Musk, was born in May 2002. But tragedy struck. At just ten weeks old, the baby died of sudden infant death syndrome, when babies suddenly and unexplainably die in their sleep. The parents were devastated. According to his wife, Musk coped by pouring himself into his work with SpaceX.

Electric Storm

While Musk worked hard to make SpaceX succeed, he kept tabs on other cutting-edge businesses. One of them

Understanding Modern Climate Change

Earth's climate has changed over time but has seen a significant warming trend since the mid-twentieth century. Human activity, such as driving gas-powered cars and cutting down large forests, has increased levels of carbon dioxide (CO_2) and other greenhouse gases in the atmosphere. These gases trap the sun's heat, leading to rising temperatures on Earth.

Scientists say Earth's average surface temperature has risen more than 2°F (1°C) since 1880. Earth's higher temperatures are strengthening hurricanes and other storms, and are causing more wildfires and droughts. Ocean temperatures are also increasing, causing polar ice to melt and sea levels to rise. According to NASA's Gravity Recovery and Climate Experiment (GRACE), Antarctica, which surrounds the South Pole, has lost an estimated 118 gigatons of ice every year since 2002. (One gigaton equals a billion metric tons.) And Greenland, which is near the North Pole, has lost an estimated 281 gigatons of ice every year.

was Tesla, a brand-new electric car company. Electric cars were not a new idea. Some of the first cars made in the 1800s ran on electricity. But gas-powered cars took over the market and dominated the automobile industry through most of the twentieth century. In the late 1990s, electric cars returned to the spotlight because they are more environmentally friendly than gas-powered cars. Electric cars, which are powered by rechargeable batteries, use less energy than gas-powered cars, and they do not emit polluting gases and particles.

Tesla's cofounders, Martin Eberhard and Marc Tarpenning, wanted to take advantage of the growing interest in eco-friendly electric cars. But they weren't just

Visitors look at a Tesla Roadster at an auto show in 2008.

interested in reducing pollution. They planned to build a high-performance, fast-as-lightning electric convertible. They called it the Roadster.

When Musk learned about the Roadster, he jumped on the Tesla bandwagon. He had long been interested in alternative energy sources, and he loved fast cars. In 2004 he invested millions of dollars in Tesla Motors and became board of directors chair and a company cofounder. Although others ran the day-to-day operations, Musk oversaw Tesla's long-term planning and overall business strategy.

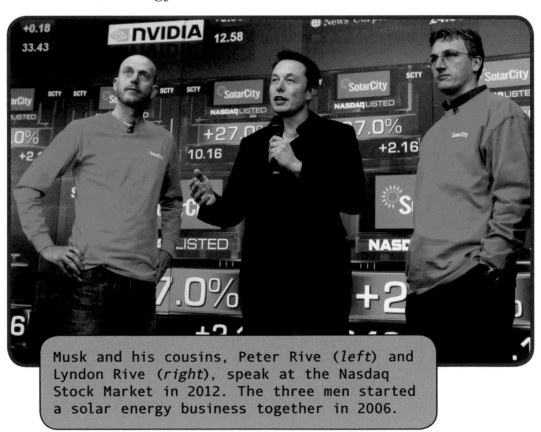

Musk and his cousins, Peter Rive (*left*) and Lyndon Rive (*right*), speak at the Nasdaq Stock Market in 2012. The three men started a solar energy business together in 2006.

Musk's family grew tremendously during this time. Twin boys, Griffin and Xavier, were born in 2004. Two years later, triplets, also boys, named Kai, Damian, and Saxon, were born. While raising his suddenly big brood, Musk also helmed two cutting-edge technology businesses. He added a third in 2006 when he helped two of his cousins, Peter and Lyndon Rive, to start SolarCity, a solar energy company. Once again, Musk was a major investor and chaired the board of directors.

Musk worked seven days a week, which didn't leave much time for his family. His marriage suffered, and the couple separated in 2008. They later divorced and agreed to share custody of their five sons.

Blast Off!

SpaceX moved to One Rocket Road in Hawthorne, California. At the new site, aerospace mechanics worked in the center of the facility and engineers sat in offices nearby. The setup allowed the two groups to work closely together, bounce ideas off of one another, and exchange quick feedback. Rather than buying parts from suppliers, the team built almost all the components they needed, including rocket engines and electronics. By bypassing outside suppliers, SpaceX saved money and ensured that everything in their rockets was top quality. Musk was driven to succeed. He often worked more than one hundred hours per week and pushed his staff to put in

On September 8, 2008, the Falcon 1 launched and orbited Earth.

similarly grueling hours.

The company's early years were marked by frustration. Some of its first rockets failed on the launchpad. Others exploded in the air. It wasn't until September 2008 that SpaceX made its first successful rocket launch, putting the Falcon 1 rocket into orbit around Earth. When that happened, the mission control team cheered. "My mind is kind of frazzled," exclaimed Musk after the rocket shot into the sky. "It's definitely one of the greatest days of my life, and probably for most people here. We've shown people we can do it. This is just the first step of many."

Further success came in December 2008, when the company won a $1.6 billion contract with NASA to make twelve supply flights to the ISS. For that, the SpaceX team designed a space capsule called Dragon. It would be able to carry not only cargo but also astronauts.

Over at Tesla, Musk and his engineers were revolutionizing the automobile business. Like SpaceX, they were building most parts from scratch rather than buying them from suppliers. The team was working on the Roadster. It was designed to go from 0 to 60 miles (0 to 97 km) an hour in less than four seconds, on par with the fastest gasoline-powered sports cars. With a fully charged battery, it would be able to travel about 250 miles (402 km)—more than many other electric cars. Car lovers were excited about the Roadster. Long before it went into production, about nine hundred buyers, including actor George Clooney and then California governor Arnold Schwarzenegger, had preordered Roadsters. The price was a whopping $109,000.

But again, the road was rocky. The Tesla team struggled with production problems and delays. And in 2008, the United States entered a severe economic recession. Tesla nearly folded that year. But a $465 million loan from the US Department of Energy enabled Tesla to stay afloat and release the Roadster.

The Roadster was followed in June 2012 by the Model S, priced at a still-high $57,400. It was unlike any other car on the market. Inside, drivers found no knobs to turn or buttons to push. Instead, they controlled everything in the car, from the headlights to the locks to the air-conditioning, via a laptoplike touch screen mounted next to the steering wheel. Instead of an internal combustion engine, power came from a giant slab of lithium ion batteries beneath the car floor.

Eco-friendly Electric Cars

Most people drive gasoline-powered cars. Run by internal combustion engines, these vehicles release polluting gases and particles into the air. But some drive electric cars, which are more eco-friendly. Electric cars run on batteries, don't emit polluting gases, and use less energy to operate than gas-powered cars.

Cleaner fuel technology can make electric cars even more eco-friendly. Musk explained, "The great thing about electric cars is that you can generate the electricity from a wide range of renewable sources like hydro [water power], geothermal [heat from inside Earth], wind, [and] solar." To fight climate change, Musk would like to see electric cars—whether built by Tesla or another company—replace gasoline-powered cars completely. He says, "Until we see every car on the road being electric, we will not stop."

Musk presents the Tesla Model S in 2009.

Drivers charged the batteries using home chargers. Away from home, they could use public charging stations that Tesla was building across California and elsewhere. Some charging stations were solar powered. A fully charged Model S could travel 300 miles (483 km) between charges. In 2013 *Motor Trend* magazine named the Model S its Car of the Year—one of the highest honors in the automotive industry. The magazine *Consumer Reports* gave the car a high rating: 99 points on a scale of 100.

As his companies prospered, Musk became richer and more famous. Some people compared him to the fictional superhero Tony Stark, a genius inventor and

billionaire who uses his Iron Man suit to fight evil. When creating the 2008 movie *Iron Man*, director Jon Favreau and lead actor Robert Downey Jr. based their version of the superhero on Musk. In *Iron Man II* in 2010, Tony Stark attends a swanky party filled with movers and shakers. One of the people he meets there is Elon Musk—played by the real Elon Musk. After that, Musk played himself in several TV shows, including *The Big Bang Theory*. He voiced his own character for the *Simpsons* episode "The Musk Who Fell to Earth."

Audiences enjoyed seeing Musk on-screen, but some coworkers found him hard to get along with. He demanded perfection from his staff. "Elon has a mind that's a bit like a calculator," said one Tesla manager.

"If you put a number on the projector that does not make sense, he will spot it." He frequently fired staffers who made mistakes—even just grammatical errors in emails. At both Tesla and SpaceX, he battled with other top executives and board members. He fought for control and eventually became the CEO of both companies.

Musk had difficulties in his private life as well. He married British actress Talulah Riley in 2010, but the relationship had many ups and downs. The couple divorced, remarried, and divorced again, officially calling it quits in 2016.

Musk and Talulah Riley in 2014

Tesla's Namesake

Tesla founders Martin Eberhard and Marc Tarpenning named their company in honor of Nikola Tesla, a Serbian American pioneer in the electrical power industry. Tesla was born in Austria-Hungary (modern-day Croatia) in 1856. After studying engineering for several years, Tesla developed a power generator that used alternating current (AC). This is an electric current that reverses direction many times each second. In the United States, inventor Thomas Edison was the first person to build electric power plants and to run electrical lines to homes and businesses. Edison's equipment ran on direct current (DC), which flows in only one direction. In 1884 Tesla moved to the United States. He tried to convince Edison and others that AC was better than DC for electrical power distribution. Tesla's AC system proved superior to DC and came into widespread use.

A newspaper story published in 1934 says that Tesla invented an electric car that ran without batteries. The story has been widely repeated, but historians say it isn't true. Tesla never built a car, but he did invent several other devices, including electric motors. He also experimented with X-rays, radar, lighting, and remote control.

Reaching for the Stars

Both Tesla and SpaceX prospered in the 2010s. Tesla introduced its most affordable car, the $35,000 Model 3. SpaceX built bigger and more powerful rockets. In May 2012 SpaceX sent the Dragon spacecraft to the ISS. It was the first private space vehicle ever to dock at the station. And in 2015 the team at SpaceX debuted perhaps the most jaw-dropping advance yet: a reusable rocket.

Up until then, space launch vehicles were used just once. After they blasted their payloads into space, their booster stages (side rockets) fell back to Earth, usually crashing into the ocean. Other stages remained out in space, orbiting Earth for years until gravity eventually pulled them down. On the trip back down through Earth's atmosphere, the rocket remains usually grew fiery hot as they rubbed against gases in the air, caught on fire, and disintegrated.

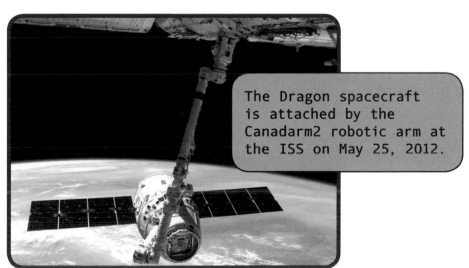

The Dragon spacecraft is attached by the Canadarm2 robotic arm at the ISS on May 25, 2012.

Musk thought it was absurd to spend millions of dollars on space equipment that was only going to crash into the ocean or burn up after one use. He explained, "The way rockets work right now is they are all expendable. So, you fly them once, and you throw it away." But with a reusable rocket, you reload fuel and fly again. Musk predicted that reusable rockets would lead to enormous cost savings: "If we could use the same Falcon 9 rocket a thousand times, then the capital costs would go from being $60 million per flight to $60,000 per flight. Obviously, that's a humongous difference."

Musk and NASA administrator Charles Bolden speak next to the Dragon spacecraft after its return to Earth on May 31, 2012.

The SpaceX engineers designed a rocket that would release its payload into space, loop around, and then fall back toward Earth in a vertical (up and down) alignment. Engines would fire to slow the rocket as it gently touched down on four 25-foot (7.6 m) landing legs. After that, the rocket could be refilled with fuel and used again. After a number of failures, SpaceX successfully landed a first-stage Falcon 9 booster rocket, first on land and then on a platform at sea, in late 2015 and early 2016. The company first reused a previously flown rocket in March 2017.

By this time, SpaceX was launching a rocket about once a month, carrying supplies for the ISS and satellites for telecommunications companies and government agencies. Tesla was also cruising at high speed. It built a giant facility in Nevada, called the Gigafactory, to produce lithium ion batteries for its cars. It planned to build more factories and vehicles, including an electric semitrailer truck that could go up to 500 miles (805 km) on a single charge.

Idea Man

Musk's home city, Los Angeles, is infamous for its crowded freeways and traffic jams. A trip that takes only fifteen minutes in light traffic can take more than an hour during rush hour. That traffic bothered Musk. So he thought of a solution. In December 2016 he founded a business called the Boring Company. Musk and other company leaders hope to build underground tunnels to enable high-speed transportation within Los Angeles and between LA and other cities. The vehicles that move through the tunnels will be similar to subway cars, but they will go much faster: about 150 miles (241 km) per hour compared with an average of 20 miles (32 km) per hour for a subway car.

In 2018 a Tesla vehicle drives into a tunnel at an event to promote the Boring Company.

For even faster transportation, Musk proposed a system called Hyperloop. It would consist of passenger pods shooting through vacuum tubes at more than 700 miles (1,127 km) per hour. Initially, engineers from Tesla and SpaceX worked on Hyperloop, but Musk wanted to involve others. He made Hyperloop an open-source project, so outside businesses can develop and build on the technology. By 2020 a number of companies and engineering teams were trying to make Hyperloop a reality.

Musk made one of his most daring proposals on September 27, 2016, at the meeting of the International Astronautical Congress in Mexico. In a speech "Making Humans a Multiplanetary Species," he announced his goal of establishing a human colony on Mars. He said that humans should become a multiplanet species, especially since climate change and other catastrophes threatened to make Earth uninhabitable. "If we were a multiplanetary species, that would reduce the possibility of some single event, man-made or natural, taking out civilization as we know it, as it did the dinosaurs," he later explained to a reporter. "It's insurance of life as we know it, and it makes the future far more inspiring if we are out there among the stars and you could move to another planet if you wanted to." He said that SpaceX would develop a craft called the Starship to fly supplies, equipment, and finally humans to Mars. As the colony grew, flights would take place once every two years, when Mars's and Earth's orbits bring the two planets closest to each other.

Also during these years, Musk spoke out against artificial intelligence, saying that machines that are more intelligent than humans could endanger civilization. He specifically worried about robotic weapons taking the place of soldiers on battlefields, making decisions about who should live and who should die without human oversight. But Musk was not against all AI. Tesla was pushing ahead on self-driving cars, which rely on artificial intelligence to make decisions in the place of human drivers. And in 2016 Musk cofounded Neuralink, which hopes to implant AI-based computer chips into human brains. This technology might help to restore eyesight, hearing, movement, or other basic functions to those with injured or impaired brains.

How to Make a Mars Colony

Musk is excited about sending humans to Mars. He said, "It's the grandest adventure I could possibly imagine. . . . I couldn't think of anything more exciting, more fun, more inspiring for the future than to have a base on Mars." But can it really be done? After all, Mars has little water, no breathable air, deadly radiation from the sun, and temperatures as low as −200°F (−129°C). So starting a colony there will be challenging. Here are just a few of the steps that we could take:

- Extract water from the icy Martian soil for drinking and growing plants.
- Turn some of the water into oxygen for breathable air.
- Build underground dwellings and greenhouses to protect colonists and plants from radiation.
- Release underground gases into the Martian atmosphere to trap heat from the sun and to raise the planet's temperature.

Many scientists say that even if all this could be done, it would take up to a thousand years to make Mars suitable for living things.

This illustration shows a potential Mars colony, including greenhouses and underground structures.

Rule Breaker

Many people called Musk a visionary. He won numerous honors, including *Inc.* magazine's Entrepreneur of the Year Award, the Heinlein Prize for Advances in Space Commercialization, the World Technology Award, the Edison Achievement Award, the Stephen Hawking Medal for Science Communication, and many others.

But other people criticized Musk. Some accused him of shady and unfair business dealings at Tesla. Others said he was actually more interested in money and power than in helping the planet with eco-friendly electric cars. Fellow scientists said that his plans for a Mars colony were based on faulty theories and were bound to fail.

Musk shrugged off the criticism and pushed ahead at both Tesla and SpaceX. But he often found himself embroiled in controversy. In the spring of 2020, for example, Musk criticized the governor of California for shutting down businesses, including his Tesla factory in Fremont, to prevent the spread of COVID-19. The highly contagious disease was then sickening millions of people around the world and killing many, especially the elderly and those with other health problems. Musk threatened to move the factory out of California to keep it operating. He then defied the state health department by reopening the plant before getting official permission. While many supported his desire to keep the factory running—and to keep paychecks coming to employees—others said that he was endangering Tesla workers by not following health department guidelines.

From left to right: Thomas Pesquet, Megan McArthur, and Shane Kimbrough, members of the SpaceX Crew-2 mission, train in 2021

On May 30 SpaceX made history once more by flying two astronauts to the ISS in its Crew Dragon spacecraft. This was the first US vehicle to carry astronauts into space since the end of the US space shuttle program in 2011. The flight ended a nearly ten-year run during which the United States had to rely on Russia's space agency to take astronauts and cargo to the ISS. It was also the first nongovernmental flight ever to carry astronauts to space.

Another positive for Musk that spring was a new baby. Since 2018 he had been dating the musician Grimes, and their son was born on May 4, 2020. They gave the boy an unusual name: X Æ A-12 Musk. Grimes explained that

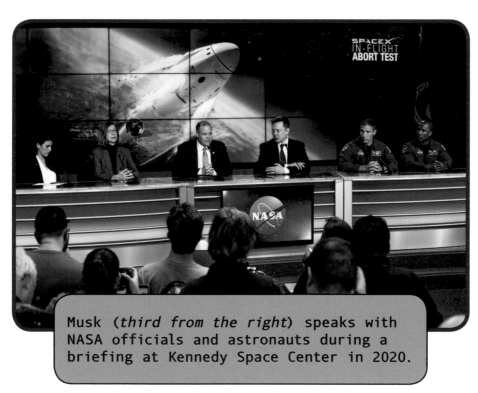

Musk (*third from the right*) speaks with NASA officials and astronauts during a briefing at Kennedy Space Center in 2020.

X stands for "the unknown variable" in math equations, Æ is an alternative spelling of AI (artificial intelligence) and means "love" in some languages, and A-12 is the model number of a sleek military spy plane. When Musk and Grimes learned that the State of California forbids numbers and symbols in personal names, they changed the name to X Æ A-Xii, using roman numerals for the number 12. It's not surprising that Musk went against the norm with his son's name. He's been breaking barriers his whole life.

Will SpaceX send missions to Mars in the 2020s? Will passengers zoom from city to city in the Hyperloop? Will electric cars completely replace those with internal combustion engines? If Elon Musk has his way, this will happen. And so far, Musk's track record of making his dreams come true is a good one.

IMPORTANT DATES

1971   Elon Musk is born in Pretoria, South Africa.

1984   Elon writes code for a sci-fi computer game called Blastar.

1989   Musk moves to Canada and enrolls in Queen's University in Ontario.

1992   Musk transfers to the University of Pennsylvania.

1995   Musk and Kimbal Musk launch Zip2, an online business directory.

1999   Musk founds the online banking company X.com, which later becomes PayPal.

2002   Musk founds SpaceX.

2004   Musk invests in Tesla Motors and chairs its board of directors.

2008   SpaceX successfully launches a rocket into orbit for the first time.

2012	Tesla introduces the Model S. SpaceX sends a Dragon spacecraft to the ISS.
2015	SpaceX lands a reusable rocket for the first time.
2016	Musk founds the Boring Company to build tunnels for underground transportation. Musk announces plans to build a human colony on Mars.
2018	SpaceX first launches its Falcon Heavy rocket, which carries a cherry-red Roadster and a dummy named Starman.
2020	SpaceX sends astronauts to the International Space Station.

SOURCE NOTES

9   Sissi Cao, "At 71, Elon Musk's Model Mom, Maye Musk, Is at Her Peak as a Style Icon," *Observer*, January 7, 2020, https://observer.com/2020/01/elon-musk-mother-maye-model-dietician -interview-book-women-self-help/.

10 Neil Strauss, "Elon Musk: The Architect of Tomorrow," *Rolling Stone*, November 15, 2017, https://www.rollingstone.com /culture/culture-features/elon-musk-the-architect-of-tomorrow -120850/.

11 Ashlee Vance, *Elon Musk: Tesla, SpaceX, and the Quest for a Fantastic Future* (New York: Ecco, 2015), 30, e-book.

17 Vance, 119.

24 Christian Davenport, *The Space Barons: Elon Musk, Jeff Bezos, and the Quest to Colonize the Cosmos* (New York: PublicAffairs, 2018), 144.

26 "Elon Musk: I'll Put a Man on Mars in 10 Years," YouTube video, 16:34, posted by *Wall Street Journal*, December 27, 2011, https://www.youtube.com/watch?v=IiPJsI8pl8Q&feature=emb_title.

26 "'Until we see every car on the road being electric, we will not stop'—Elon Musk," YouTube video, 0:23, posted by Mark Sita, March 4, 2019, https://www.youtube.com/watch?v=bqf26thSK7Q.

28–29 Vance, *Elon Musk*, 220.

32 Davenport, *Space Barons*, 198.

32 Stephen L. Petranek, *How We'll Live on Mars* (New York: Simon and Schuster, 2015), 33, e-book.

35 Strauss, "Elon Musk."

37 "Elon Musk 'Mars Pioneer Award' Acceptance Speech—15th Annual International Mars Society Convention," YouTube video, 33:00, posted by the Mars Society, August 9, 2012, https://www.youtube.com/watch?v=PK0kTcJFnVk&feature=emb_title.

SELECTED BIBLIOGRAPHY

Belfiore, Michael. "Behind the Scenes with the World's Most Ambitious Rocket Makers." *Popular Mechanics*, September 1, 2009. https://www.popularmechanics.com/space/rockets/a5073/4328638/.

Blystone, Dan. "How Elon Musk Became Elon Musk: A Brief Biography." Investopedia. Last modified March 4, 2020. https://www.investopedia.com/articles/personal-finance/061015/how-elon-musk-became-elon-musk.asp.

Davenport, Christian. *The Space Barons: Elon Musk, Jeff Bezos, and the Quest to Colonize the Cosmos.* New York: PublicAffairs, 2018.

Gunter, Joel. "Elon Musk: The Man Who Sent His Sports Car into Space." BBC News, February 10, 2018. https://www.bbc.com/news/science-environment-42992143.

Keats, Robin. "Rocket Man." *Queen's Alumni Review*, no. 1 (2013). https://www.queensu.ca/gazette/alumnireview/stories/rocket-man.

Niedermeyer, Edward. *Ludicrous: The Unvarnished Story of Tesla Motors.* Dallas: BenBella Books, 2019.

Petranek, Stephen L. *How We'll Live on Mars.* New York: Simon and Schuster, 2015. e-book.

Strauss, Neil. "Elon Musk: The Architect of Tomorrow," *Rolling Stone*, November 15, 2017, https://www.rollingstone.com/culture/culture-features/elon-musk-the-architect-of-tomorrow-120850/.

Vance, Ashlee. *Elon Musk: Tesla, SpaceX, and the Quest for a Fantastic Future.* New York: Ecco, 2015, e-book.

LEARN MORE

Alternative Energy
https://c03.apogee.net/mvc/home/hes/land/el?utilityname=gru&spc=k
ids&tid=16183

Hirsch, Rebecca E. *Mysteries of Mars*. Minneapolis: Lerner Publications, 2021.

Kurtz, Kevin. *Climate Change and Rising Temperatures*. Minneapolis: Lerner Publications, 2019.

Milligan, Aiyanna. *Cutting-Edge SpaceX News*. Minneapolis: Lerner Publications, 2020.

NASA for Students in 5th to 8th Grades
https://www.nasa.gov/stem/forstudents/5-8/index.html

Safe Return
https www.timeforkids.com/g56/safe-return/

INDEX

artificial intelligence (AI), 9, 36

Boring Company, 34

climate change, 20, 26, 35
computer language, 11–12

Dragon spacecraft, 24, 31, 40

Eberhard, Martin, 21, 30
electric cars, 21, 25–26, 38, 41

Falcon Heavy, 7–8
Falcon 1, 24

Hyperloop, 35

International Astronautical Congress, 35
International Space Station (ISS), 8, 24, 31, 33, 40

Los Angeles, CA, 16, 33–34

Mars colony, 16, 35, 37–38
Mueller, Tom, 18
Musk, Kimbal, 9–10, 12
Musk, Nevada Alexander, 19
Musk, X Æ A-Xii, 40

National Aeronautics and Space Administration (NASA), 18, 24

PayPal, 16

Queen's University, 12

reusable rocket, 31–32
Riley, Talulah, 29
Roadster, 8, 22, 25

Silicon Valley, 12, 14, 16
SolarCity, 23
South Africa, 9–10, 12

Tarpenning, Marc, 21, 30
Tesla, Nikola, 30

University of Pennsylvania, 13–14
University of Pretoria, 12

Wilson, Justine, 12–13, 16, 19, 23